LET'S SHARE A HAIR STORY

SHAWNTA SMITH SAYNER

With an approach dedicated to supporting self-love, self-care, diversity, and inclusion, the Let's Share series empowers us to communicate, care, and connect!
Collect them all!

*For my friends who are family,
and my family who are friends.*

With my

proud crown,

I can do it all!

or stand it tall.

I can braid a **maze,**
or form soft **puffs.**

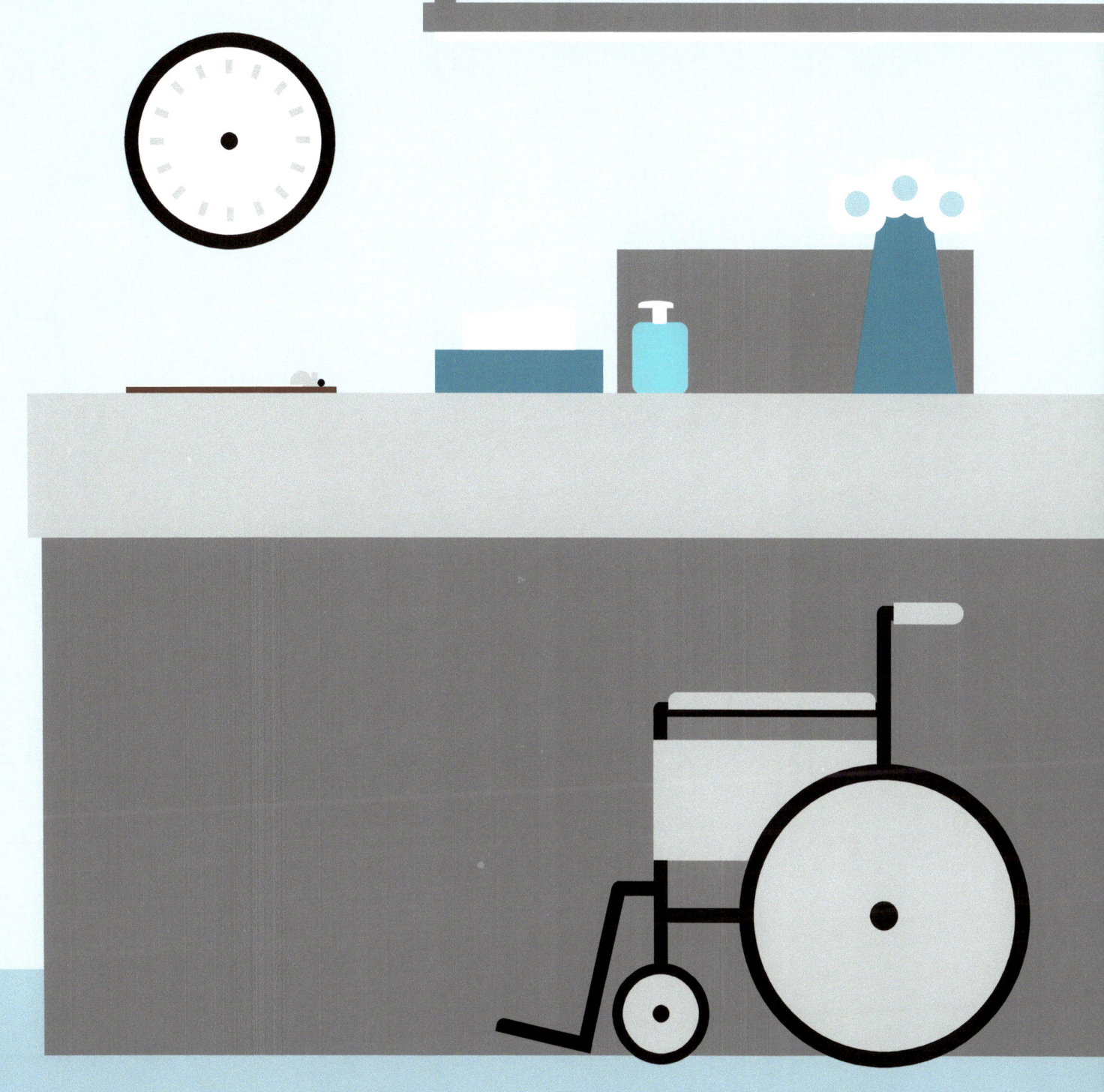

I can try some **bangs** to frame my **eyes**.

I can wear it **natural** as can be.

Also **shape** it with all **kinds** of things.

I can add **barrettes**,
bands, **bows**,
or **beads**.

Right now, and in the future, too,

whichever way I wear my 'do,

I wonder who I'll dare to be...

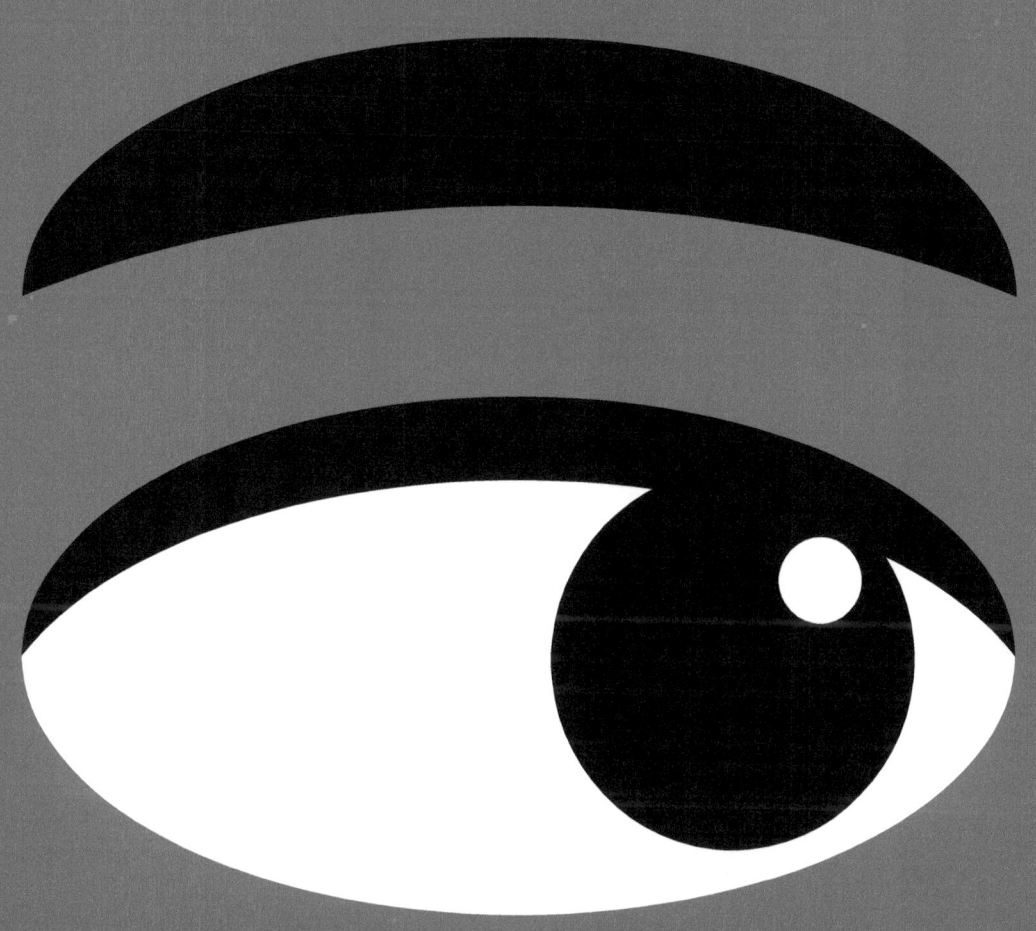

Shawnta Smith Sayner is an educator, caregiver, and lifelong learning advocate who supports students, faculty, and families alike, working in schools and traveling as a guest speaker. Known for *WeAreTeachers'* "15 Ways to Bring More Positive Language into Your Classroom and School," Shawnta's passions extend to supporting wellness, diversity, and inclusion throughout communities. Shawnta lives with her beautifully multicultural family near Milwaukee, WI.

Also by Shawnta Smith Sayner:
Let's Share a Superhero Story
Let's Share a Hope Story
Let's Share a Holiday Story

For freebies, updates, and more, please visit www.shawntasmithsayner.com.

Copyright © 2020 by Shawnta Smith Sayner

All rights reserved. Published by Inclusive Books & More, Brookfield, WI. No part of this publication may be reproduced, stored in a retrieval system, or transmitted in any form or by any means, electronic, mechanical, photocopying, recording, or otherwise, without written permission of the copyright holder. For information regarding permission, contact the publisher through its website: www.inclusivebooksandmore.com.

This book is a work of creative nonfiction. Names, characters, places, and incidents are either the product of the author's imagination or are used fictitiously. Any resemblance to actual persons, living or dead, business establishments, events, or locales is entirely coincidental.

Library of Congress Cataloging-in-Publication Data available / Library of Congress Control Number: 2020911631
ISBN: 978-1-952944-08-6 (hc) / ISBN: 978-1-952944-00-0 (pb) / ISBN: 978-1-952944-01-7 (eb)

First Edition: July 2020